A Touch of Friendship

By Diane Voreis

Cover Illustration and Typography by
MarketForce, Burr Ridge, IL

Published by Great Quotations Publishing Company
2800 Centre Circle
Downers Grove, IL 60515, U.S.A.

Library of Congress Catalog Number: 98-75445

ISBN 1-56245-353-X

Printed in Hong Kong 2001

Dedication:

This is for my friends and especially for my mother, Frances, whose friendship has brightened my days.

There are those who pass like ships in the night.
Who meet for a moment, then sail out of sight
with never a backwards glance of regret; folks
we know briefly then quickly forget. Then
there are friends who sail together through
quiet waters and stormy weather helping each
other through joy and through strife. And they
are the kind who give meaning to life.

4

A real friend warms you by his presence, trusts you with his secrets, and remembers you in his prayers.

5

We have been friends together;
In sunshine and in shade.

Caroline Norton

*Gratitude preserves old friendships,
and procures new.*

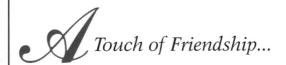 *Touch of Friendship...*

> *Take time and enjoy the sun, the
> breeze and the water. Go for a
> leisurely boat ride on a nice
> summer's day with a friend*

8

I think if it's at all possible, your best friend and you owe it to each other to make some space just to be alone together again. That way, you can talk about what you were, and that feels good. You can also talk about what you are - that's trickier, but if you're lucky, that feels good too.

Elizabeth Berg

A true friend is the greatest of all blessings and the one which we take the least thought to acquire.

Francois, Duc de La Rochefoucald

Friends are my heart and my ears.

Michael Jordan

There's a special kind of freedom friends enjoy.
Freedom to share innermost thoughts, to ask
a favor, to show their true feelings.
The freedom to simply be themselves.

We cannot tell the precise moment when a friendship is formed. As in filling a vessel drop by drop, there is at last a drop that makes it run over; so in a series of kindnesses, there is a last one that makes the heart run over.

Samuel Johnson

Who seeks a friend without a fault
remains without one.

Proverb

14

The true source of cheerfulness is benevolence. The soul that perpetually overflows with kindness and sympathy will always be cheerful.

P. Goodwin

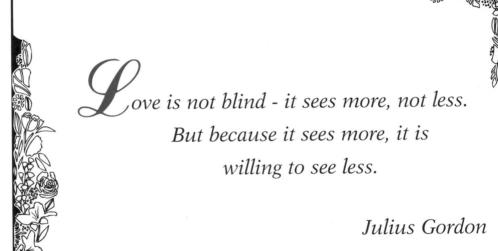

Love is not blind - it sees more, not less.
But because it sees more, it is
willing to see less.

Julius Gordon

16

One of the sanest, surest and most generous joys of life comes from being happy over the good fortune of others.

Archibald Rutledge

ake time for friends... it is the source of happiness.

A word or even a nod from one who loves us carries a lot of weight.

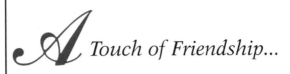 *Touch of Friendship...*

*Journey with your friend to a
quaint tea shop to enjoy an
afternoon of soothing tea, delicious
scones and warm conversation.*

20

You will find, as you look back upon your life, that the moments that stand out are the moments when you have done things for others.

Henry Drummond

Treat your friends as you do your pictures, and place them in their best light.

Jennie Jerome Churchill

*Each friend represents a world
in us, a world possible not born
until they arrive, and it is only by this
meeting that a new world is born.*

Anais Nin

One is taught by experience to put a premium on those few people who can appreciate you for what you are.

Gail Goodwin

The most I can do for my friend is singly to be his friend. I have no wealth to bestow on him. If he knows that I am happy in loving him, he will want no other reward. Is not friendship divine in this?

Henry David Thoreau

 *Touch of Friendship...*

*Spend a day of culture with your friend
and visit an art museum to view and
discuss an art exhibition.*

26

*Friendships aren't perfect and yet
they are very precious.*

Letty Cottin Pogrebin

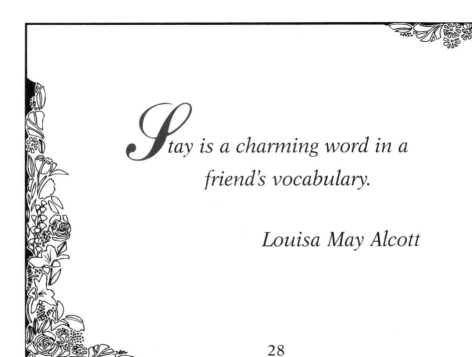

Stay is a charming word in a friend's vocabulary.

Louisa May Alcott

You give but little when you give of your possessions. It is when you give of yourself that you truly give.

Kahil Gibran

True friends don't sympathize with your weakness - they help summon your strength.

Friendship is a living thing that lasts only as long as it is nourished with kindness, sympathy, and understanding.

It's that person you call when you're feeling down, that person who will listen to you when you have nothing to say. You know, that friend who you can go six months without speaking to and then you pick up the phone, hear her voice - and it seems like only yesterday since you last spoke.

Oprah Winfrey

32

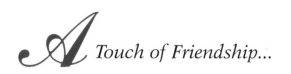 *Touch of Friendship...*

Call a friend that you haven't spoken to for a while to just say "Hi" and to let her know that you've been thinking about her.

33

A faithful friend in time of adversity is of all other most comfortable.

The balm of life, a kind and faithful friend.

y friendship, like wine, improves as time advances. And may we always have old wine, old friends, and young cares.

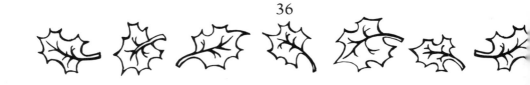

Chance makes our parents, but choice makes our friends.

Jacques Delille

True friendship comes when silence between two people is comfortable.

Dave Tyson Gentry

*It's important to our friends to believe
that we are unreservedly frank with
them, and important to friendship
that we are not.*

Mignon McLaughlin

Friendship is a serious affection; the most sublime of all affections: because it is founded on principle and cemented by time.

Mary Wollstonecraft

You measure a friend by the breadth of his understanding, I mean that delicate response from the chords of feeling which is involuntary.

D. H. Lawrence

A good friend can tell you what is the matter with you in a minute.

Arthur Brisbane

Touch of Friendship...

Have a dessert party and invite friends over for scrumptious desserts, coffee, and good conversation.

Life is to be fortified by many friendships - to love and to be loved is the greatest happiness of existence.

Sydney Smith

44

The friendships which last are those wherein each friend respects the other's dignity to the point of not really wanting anything from him.

Cyril Connolly

Two persons will not be friends long if they cannot forgive each other's little failings.

H. Jean De La Bruyer

46

Friendship is like a sheltering tree.

Coleridge

*W*hen a friend is in trouble don't annoy him by asking him if there is anything you can do. Think up something appropriate and do it.

E. W. Howe

A Touch of Friendship...

Cheer up a friend who's ill with a dose of sunshine.
Create your own Get Well basket with some fresh
flowers, chicken soup, and a good book to read.

49

The essence of true friendship is to make allowances for another's little lapses.

David Storey

*riendship with oneself is all important,
because without it one cannot be
friends with anyone else in the world.*

Eleanor Roosevelt

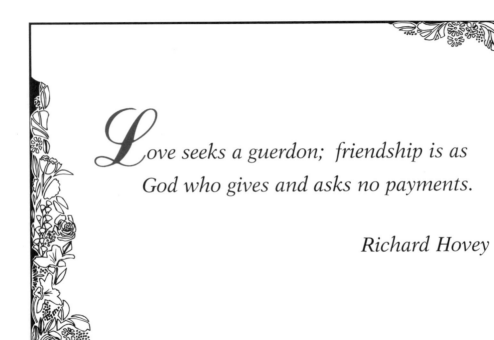

*Love seeks a guerdon; friendship is as
God who gives and asks no payments.*

Richard Hovey

52

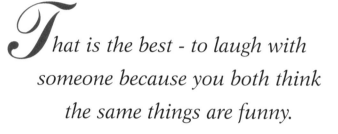

That is the best - to laugh with someone because you both think the same things are funny.

Gloria Vanderbilt

A Touch of Friendship...

Tell the best jokes that you've heard recently to your friend. Share the wonderful gift of laughter.

54

The ornaments of a house are the friends who visit it.

always felt that the great high privilege, relief, and comfort of friendship was that one had to explain nothing.

Katherine Mansfield

There was a definite process by which one made people into friends, and it involved talking to them and listening to them for hours at a time.

Rebecca West

*Trouble is a sieve through which
we sift our acquaintances.
Those too big to pass through
are our friends.*

Arlene Francis

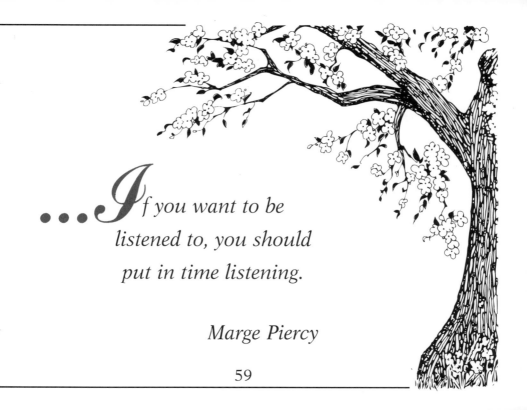

...If you want to be listened to, you should put in time listening.

Marge Piercy

*It is wise to apply the oil of refined
politeness to the mechanism of friendship.*

Colette

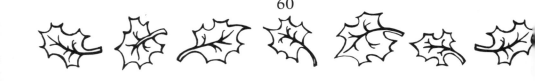

*Let us always meet each other with a smile,
for the smile is the beginning of love.*

Mother Teresa

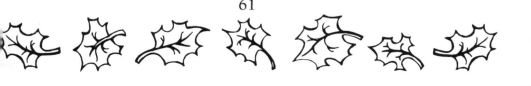

*Without friends, no one would choose
to live, though he had all other goods.*

Aristotle

We cannot really love anybody
with whom we never laugh.

Agnes Repplier

A Touch of Friendship...

*Pamper your friend. Plan a trip to a
day spa together and get new
hair cuts and manicures.*

64

*A good friend knows when to listen, truly
listen to hear the outpourings of your
heart without comment.*

Friends can turn everyday occasions into celebrations just by their presence.

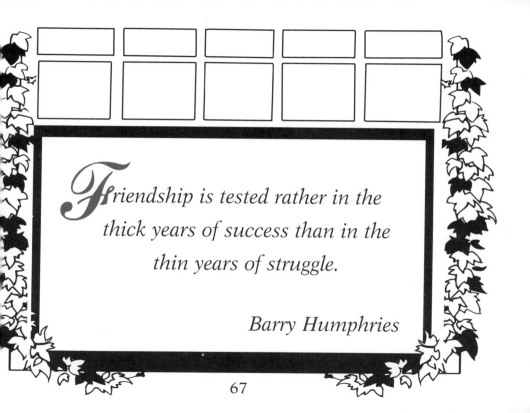

Friendship is tested rather in the thick years of success than in the thin years of struggle.

Barry Humphries

If we would build on a sure foundation in friendship, we must love our friends for their sake rather than for our own.

Charlotte Brontë

Do not keep the alabaster boxes of your love and tenderness sealed up until your friends are dead. Fill their lives with sweetness. Speak approvingly cheerful words while their ears can hear them and while their hearts can be thrilled by them.

Harriet Beecher Stowe

A Touch of Friendship...

Girlfriends just wanna have fun!
Go rollerblading or try a new
sport activity with your friends.

*When you make a world tolerable
for yourself you make a world
tolerable for others.*

Anais Nin

*o distance of place or lapse of time can
lessen the friendship of those who are
thoroughly persuaded of each other's worth.*

Robert Southey

The first duty of love is to listen.

Paul Tillich

You are unique, and if that is not fulfilled, then something has been lost.

Martha Graham

Friendship needs no words - it is
solitude delivered from the
anguish of loneliness.

Dag Hammarskjold

he reward of friendship is itself. The man who does hope for anything else does not understand what true friendship is.

Saint Ailred of Rievaulx

A Touch of Friendship...

> *Surprise your friend with a colorful*
> *balloon bouquet at work to*
> *brighten her birthday.*

*Good friendships are fragile things
and require as much care as any
other fragile and precious things.*

Randolph Bourne

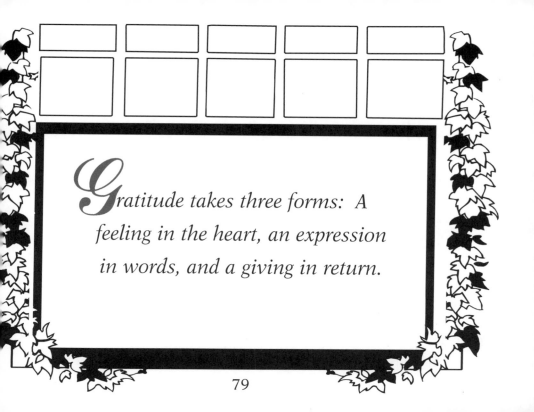

*G*ratitude takes three forms: A
feeling in the heart, an expression
in words, and a giving in return.

79

Without friendship and the openness and trust that go with it, skills are barren and knowledge may become an unguided missile.

Frank H. T. Rhodes

The happiest business in all the world is that of making friends,

     And no investment on the street pays larger dividends,

For life is more than stocks and bonds, and love than rate percent.

And he who gives in friendship's name shall reap what he has spent.

Anne S. Eaton

The finest kind of friendship is between people who expect a great deal of each other but never ask it.

Sylvia Bremer

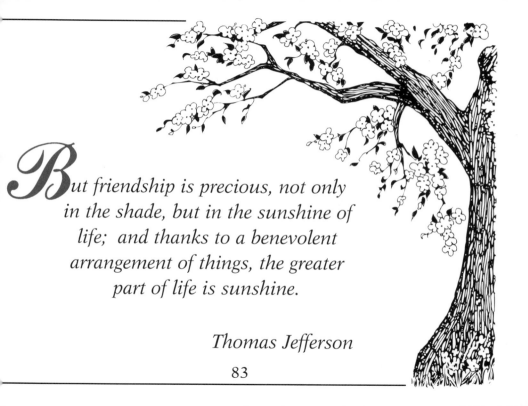

But friendship is precious, not only in the shade, but in the sunshine of life; and thanks to a benevolent arrangement of things, the greater part of life is sunshine.

Thomas Jefferson

eing a good friend, and having a good friend, can enrich your days and bring you lifelong satisfaction. But friendships don't just happen. They have to be created and nurtured. Like another skill, building friendship has to be practiced.

Sue Browder

A Touch of Friendship...

Sew, paint, needlepoint...create an heirloom with your own hands and heart for that special friend.

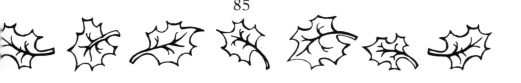

The worth of a kind deed lies in the love that inspires it.

The Talmud

The wise man does not permit himself to set up even in his own mind any comparison of his friends. His friendship is capable of going to extremes with many people, evoked as it is by many qualities.

Charles Dudley Warner

I found real love in girlfriends... I've always found girls I've loved and who've made me laugh...a really good friendship.

Tina Turner

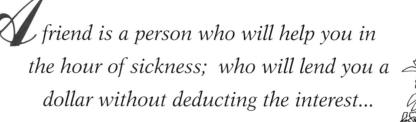

A friend is a person who will help you in the hour of sickness; who will lend you a dollar without deducting the interest...

Dorothy C. Retsloff

$\mathcal{F}$riendship is honey...
but don't eat it all.

Moroccan Proverb

We find rest in those we love, and we provide a resting place in ourselves for those who love us.

Saint Bernard of Clairvaux

It is the privilege of loving to be aware of a curtain's fold or the intonation of a human voice, to be acutely, agonizingly conscious of the moment that's always present and always passing.

Marya Mannes

*O*ne friend, one person who is truly
understanding, who takes the trouble
to listen to us as we consider our
problem, can change our whole
outlook on the world.

Dr. Elton Mayo

Love is but the discovery of ourselves in others, and the delight in the recognition.

Alexander Smith

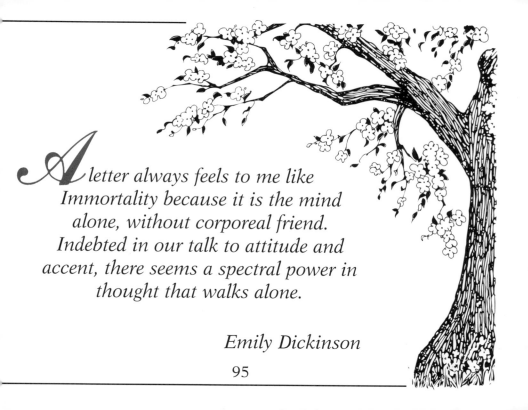

*A letter always feels to me like
Immortality because it is the mind
alone, without corporeal friend.
Indebted in our talk to attitude and
accent, there seems a spectral power in
thought that walks alone.*

Emily Dickinson

The true use of a letter is to let one know that one is remembered and valued.

Vincent McNabb

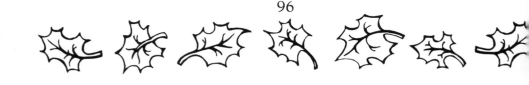

A Touch of Friendship...

Write a letter to your friend letting her know
how much she is appreciated and how you
value her friendship.

The greatest healing therapy is friendship and love.

Hubert Humphrey

A kind word is like a Spring day.

Russian Proverb

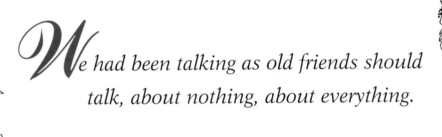

We had been talking as old friends should talk, about nothing, about everything.

Lillian Hellman

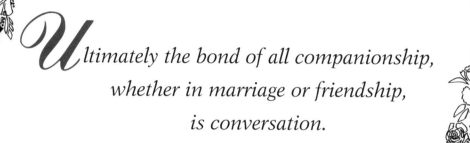

Ultimately the bond of all companionship,
whether in marriage or friendship,
is conversation.

Oscar Wilde

A Touch of Friendship...

Have a World of Good Taste party... with foods from around the world. Involve your friends with a progressive dinner party.

The moment that one can talk about things, that moment they become bearable, one sees them in the right light.

A. C. Benson

riendships, like marriages, are dependent on avoiding the unforgivable.

John D. MacDonald

This is the art of courage: to see things as they are and still believe that victory lies not with those who avoid the bad, but those who taste, in living awareness, every drop of the good.

Victoria Lincoln

Many a friendship, long, loyal, and self-sacrificing, rested at first on no thicker a foundation than a kind word.

Frederick W. Faber

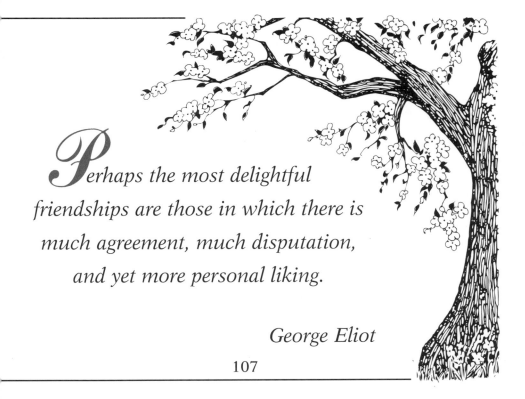

*Perhaps the most delightful
friendships are those in which there is
much agreement, much disputation,
and yet more personal liking.*

George Eliot

It is not what you give your friend, but what you are willing to give him, that determines the quality of friendship.

Mary Dixon Thayer

108

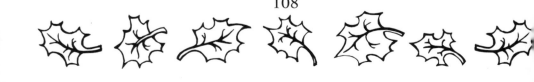

Friendship adds a brighter radiance to prosperity, and lightens the burden of adversity by dividing and sharing it.

Cicero

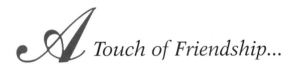 Touch of Friendship...

Start a tradition of giving a memorable
holiday ornament each year to your friend.

Of all the gifts that a wise providence grants us to make life full and happy, friendship is the most beautiful.

Epicurus

The holy passion of Friendship is as of so sweet and steady and loyal and enduring a nature that it will last through a whole lifetime, if not asked to lend money.

Mark Twain

112

Spread cheer each and every day
by making new friends along the way.
A simple smile, a hearty hello
are the kind gestures to show
and to greet everyone we meet.

Diane Voreis

113

Happy is the house that shelters a friend.

Ralph Waldo Emerson

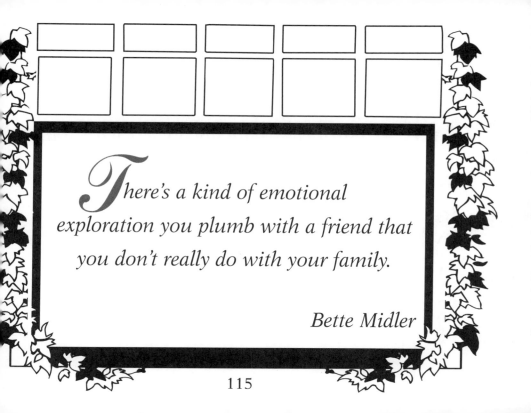

There's a kind of emotional exploration you plumb with a friend that you don't really do with your family.

Bette Midler

There isn't much that I can do,
But I can share my flowers with you,
And I can share my books with you,
And sometimes share your burdens, too...
As on our way we go.

Maude V. Preston

116

*Surely we ought to prize those friends
on whose principles and opinions we
may constantly rely of whom we may
say in all emergencies,
"I know what they would think."*

Hannah Farnham Lee

It's the friends that you can call up at 4 a.m. that matter.

Marlene Dietrich

*Friendship is an art,
and very few persons are born
with a natural gift for it.*

Kathleen Norris

riendship requires great communication between friends. Otherwise, it can neither be born, nor exist.

Saint Francis De Sales

120

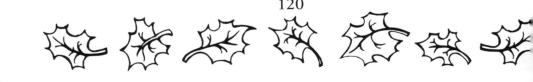

Celebrate the happiness that friends are always giving.
Make every day a holiday and celebrate just living.

Amanda Bradley

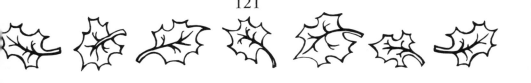

A Touch of Friendship...

*Celebrate unique and unusual
occasions like Ground Hog's Day
with your friends.*

A friend sees in you all possibilities, perhaps even the ones you've forgotten that you possess.

The supreme happiness of life is the conviction that we are loved; loved for ourselves, or rather, loved in spite of ourselves.

Victor Hugo

124

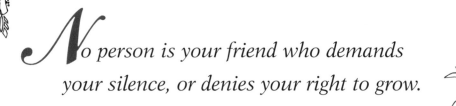

No person is your friend who demands your silence, or denies your right to grow.

Alice Walker

Wishing to be friends is quick work, but friendship is a slow-ripening fruit.

Aristotle

Like rainbows and flowers,
friends brighten hours.

It seems to me that one privilege of friendship is "to quench the fiery darts of the wicked," to make the best of friends, to encourage and believe in them, to hand on the pleasant things.

A. C. Benson

I think, from some brief experience of the thing, that as friendships grow old, they seem to depend less on actual contacts and messages in order to maintain their soundness; the growth has got into the wood of the tree, and is there; and yet I am also quite sure that no friendship yields its true pleasure and nobility of nature without frequent communication, sympathy and service.

George E. Woodberry

here is a purifying power in laughter - both for individuals and for nations.

Lin Yutang

A Touch of Friendship...

Enjoy the earlier joys of childhood with your friends by making S'mores and singing favorite songs on a pleasant summer's eve.

131

Blessed are they who have the gift of making friends
for it is one of God's best gifts. It involves many things
but above all, the power of going out of one's self, and
appreciating whatever is noble and loving in another.

Thomas Hughes

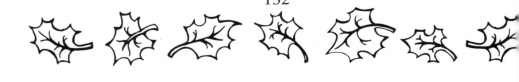

Genuine friendship is like sound health, it's value is seldom known until it is lost.

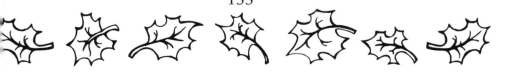

Friendship is a strong and habitual inclination in two persons to promote the goodness and happiness of one another.

Eustace Budgell

Kindness is the oil that takes the friction out of life.

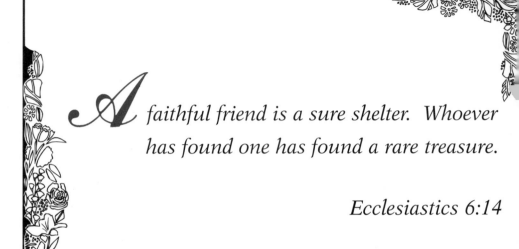

A faithful friend is a sure shelter. Whoever has found one has found a rare treasure.

Ecclesiastics 6:14

136

Friends are relatives you make for yourself.

Eustache Deschamps

The only way to have a friend
is to be one.

Ralph Waldo Emerson

A Touch of Friendship...

Be a friend to someone today with a warm smile, a listening ear and an open heart.

Human beings are born into this span of life of which the best thing is its friendships and intimacies, and soon their places will know them no more, and yet they leave their friendships and intimacies with no cultivation, to grow as they will by the roadside, expecting them to "keep" by force of mere inertia.

William James

140

Friendship is a living thing that lasts only as long as it is nourished with kindness, sympathy, and understanding.

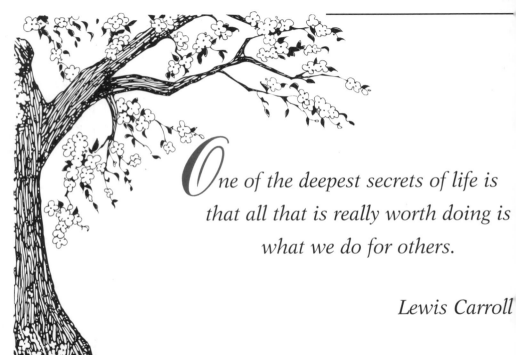

One of the deepest secrets of life is that all that is really worth doing is what we do for others.

Lewis Carroll

Appreciation is the heart's memory.

*To fall down you manage alone, but
it takes friendly hands to get up.*

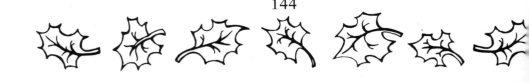

*It is said that love is blind. Friendship,
on the other hand is clairvoyant.*

Philip Soupault

Friendship of a kind that cannot easily be reversed tomorrow must have its roots in common interests and shared beliefs.

Barbara Tuchman

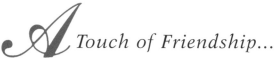 *Touch of Friendship...*

*Learn something new and fun together
with a friend. Be creative...take a dance,
painting or art class, learn to speak
a foreign language, sign up for gourmet
cooking classes.
Expand your horizons and interests.*

147

Gratitude preserves old friendships, and procures new.

148

A true friend is someone who says nice things behind your back.

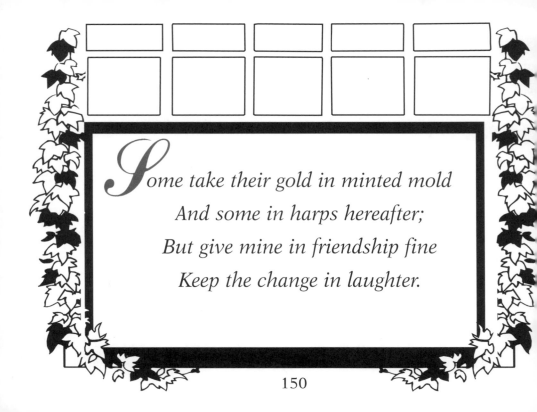

Some take their gold in minted mold
And some in harps hereafter;
But give mine in friendship fine
Keep the change in laughter.

150

A home-made friend wears longer than one you buy in the market.

Austin O'Malley

There's a special kind of freedom friends enjoy. Freedom to share innermost thoughts, to ask a favor, to show their true feelings. The freedom to simply be themselves.

152

Whether sixty or sixteen, there is in every human being's heart the love of wonder, the sweet amazement at the stars and starlike things, the undaunted challenge of events, the unfailing childlike appetite for what-next, and the joy of the game of living.

Samuel Ullman

153

*Friendships that have stood
the test of time and change
are surely best.*

Joseph Parry

A Touch of Friendship...

*Celebrate the anniversary date
of the start of your friendship.*

*Spend a new penny on an old friend,
share an old pleasure with a new friend
and lift up the heart of a true friend
by writing his name on the wings of a dragon.*

Chinese Proverb

She is a friend to my mind...the pieces I am, she gathers them and gives them back to me in all the right order. It's good when you got a woman who is a friend of your mind.

Toni Morrison

We take care of our health, we lay up money, we make our roof tight, and our clothing sufficient, but who provides wisely that he shall not be wanting in the best property of all -- friends?

Ralph Waldo Emerson

*riends, books, a cheerful heart, and
conscience clear are the most choice
companions we have here.*

William Mather

If we don't have friends,
then I ain't got nothing.

Billie Holiday

I have three chairs in my house: one for
solitude, two for friendship, three for company.

Henry David Thoreau

*H*old a true friend with
both your hands.

Nigerian Proverb

Sooner or later you've heard what all your best friends have to say. Then comes the tolerance of real love.

Ned Borem

Oh the comfort, the inexpressible comfort, of feeling safe with a person, having neither to weigh thoughts nor measure words, but pouring them all right out, just as they are, chaff and grain together; certain that a faithful hand will take and sift them, keep them, keep what is worth keeping, and with the breath of kindness, blow the rest away.

Rex Cole

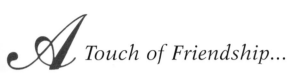 *Touch of Friendship...*

Plant seeds of friendship. When friends move away give them a present of flower bulbs to plant at their new home. The beautiful blooms will brighten their day and remind them of you.

165

The only thing to do is hug one's friends tight and do one's job.

Edith Wharton

166

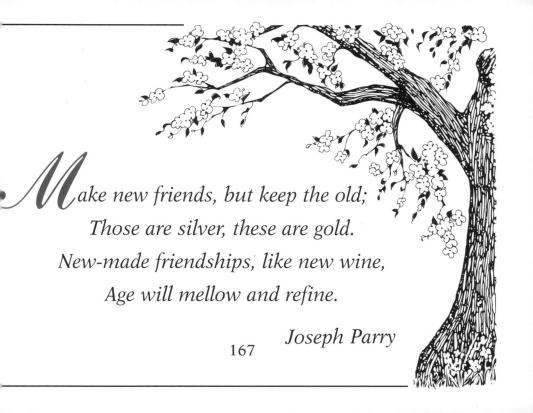

Make new friends, but keep the old;
Those are silver, these are gold.
New-made friendships, like new wine,
Age will mellow and refine.

Joseph Parry

167

Other Titles by Great Quotations

301 Ways to Stay Young At Heart
African-American Wisdom
A Lifetime of Love
A Light Heart Lives Long
Angel-grams
As A Cat Thinketh
A Servant's Heart
Astrology for Cats
Astrology for Dogs
A Teacher is Better Than Two Books
A Touch of Friendship
Can We Talk
Celebrating Women
Chicken Soup
Chocoholic Reasonettes
Daddy & Me
Dare to Excel
Erasing My Sanity
Falling in Love
Fantastic Father, Dependable Dad
Golden Years, Golden Words
Graduation Is Just The Beginning
Grandma, I Love You
Happiness is Found Along The Way

High Anxieties
Hooked on Golf
I Didn't Do It
Ignorance is Bliss
I'm Not Over the Hill
Inspirations
Interior Design for Idiots
Let's Talk Decorating
Life's Lessons
Life's Simple Pleasures
Looking for Mr. Right
Midwest Wisdom
Mommy & Me
Mom's Homemade Jams
Mother, I Love You
Motivating Quotes for Motivated People
Mrs. Murphy's Laws
Mrs. Webster's Dictionary
My Daughter, My Special Friend
Only a Sister
Parenting 101
Pink Power
Read the Fine Print

Reflections
Romantic Rhapsody
Size Counts !
Social Disgraces
Sports Prose
Stress or Sanity
The ABC's of Parenting
The Be-Attitudes
The Birthday Astrologer
The Cornerstones of Success
The Rose Mystique
The Secret Language of Men
The Secret Language of Women
The Secrets in Your Face
The Secrets in Your Name
TeenAge of Insanity
Thanks from the Heart
The Lemonade Handbook
The Mother Load
The Other Species
Wedding Wonders
Words From The Coach
Working Woman's World

Great Quotations Publishing Company
2800 Centre Circle
Downers Grove, IL 60515, U.S.A.
Phone: 630-268-9900   Fax: 630-268-9500